RECOGNIZING WHEN GOD SPEAKS

I0616115

A JOURNEY INTO HOW THE LORD USES US TO GUIDE, AFFIRM AND REVEAL HIS WILL

Jacquatta Jackson Jones, Psy.D.

RECOGNIZING WHEN GOD SPEAKS

Copyright © 2025 by Jacquatta Jackson Jones

ISBN: 979-8-218-70411-7

Printed in the United States of America

Published by: Power of Meditation in God's

Presence

Before You Begin

A Heart Posture for the Journey Ahead

"Seek the LORD and His strength; seek His face evermore". – Psalm 105:4

This book is not written to simply pursue the hand of God - what He can provide or do, but to draw you toward His face—who He is.

To truly know God is to come into the revelation of your identity.

We are spirit beings, created in His image (Genesis 1:26), shaped from the dust of the earth (Genesis 2:7), and endowed with a living soul. This divine design is not accidental—it is intentional.

As you read, keep your heart fixed on the Word of God. Let it center you, challenge you, and confirm the truth of who you are in Him.

And may you be stirred to encourage those who have yet to discover their identity and divine purpose on this earth. You were created on purpose—begin this journey with expectation.

Dedication

To the one and only true God, who created me on purpose and for purpose.

This book is dedicated to the God who speaks—the Author of every dream and the Giver of divine assignments.

May every word written reflect the truth that each of us was designed with intentionality, equipped with unique gifts, and called to impact the world in ways that echo eternity.

To every reader searching for meaning: your purpose is not random—it is God-given.

Believe in Him!

Scripture Dedication

Jeremiah 33:3 King James Version

"Call unto me, and I will answer thee, and shew thee great and mighty things, which thou knowest not."

Jeremiah 33:3 Amplified Version

"Call to Me and I will answer you and tell you (and even show you) great and mighty things, (things which have been confined and hidden), which you do not know and understand and cannot distinguish."

TABLE OF CONTENTS

FOREWORD

Recognizing When God Speaks is not just a book about dreams, but a journey into understanding how a supernatural God speaks to us in supernatural ways.

The personal stories and biblical truths shared by Dr. Jacquatta J. Jones will provide revelation and insight into the God of light that speaks at night.

This book is both for the new believer who wonders at times if their dreams are just dreams or if they are God trying to tell them something. This book will also encourage the mature believer to hold on to and have faith and know that God will reveal what needs to be revealed.

I met Dr. Jones around 1996 and have watched her grow tremendously in the Lord because of an insatiable hunger for God. Not for what was in His hand, but for every word that flows from His mouth. (Matt.4:4)

Her love for God is sincere as much as it is pure. My prayer is that everything God is to her, He will be to you as you discover how to recognize when God speaks.

In His Service Because of His Love,
Dr. Tony Jones, MTh. Psy.D. (Husband)

PREFACE

Dreams have always fascinated me, not just as fleeting images of the night but as divine whispers that can shape our waking lives. This book was birthed from years of personal encounters with God through dreams, along with countless conversations with others who have experienced His voice, not only in dreams but also through visions, meditation, His word, songs, and that precious, still, small voice. It's not merely a collection of stories; it's a testimony to the God who still speaks.

I don't come to you as a scholar of dreams or a professional interpreter, but as a friend of Christ, an ordained minister, counselor, wife, mother, and spiritual mentor. I've spent years walking alongside others through life's joys and challenges, often finding that God meets us most powerfully when we lay down to rest.

This book is written for those who sense that their experiences mean more than they appear. It's for the curious, the questioning, and the spiritually hungry.

My prayer is that as you turn these pages, you'll begin to see your encounters not as random but as purposeful. May your spiritual eyes, ears, and sense of smell be opened to the gentle, powerful voice of the One (Holy Spirit) who speaks, even in the stillness of the night.

INTRODUCTION

I first began to completely recognize one of the gifts God placed within me when I was just a little girl. Back then, I didn't have the words or wisdom to describe it, I only knew that something unusual was happening. I had a recurring dream that left me deeply afraid. In the dream, the sky was always a beautiful shade of blue, dotted with soft, gentle clouds. Yet something was falling toward me from above, and I would wake up terrified, not understanding what it meant.

For a long time, the dream made no sense. But now, looking back, I believe it was the beginning of God revealing a spiritual gift inside of me. I've come to understand that the Lord often shows glimpses of our purpose little by little, because if He revealed it all at once, we wouldn't be able to carry the weight of it.

Our purpose is too important to be rushed. And sometimes, it begins with something as simple and as mysterious as a dream.

Chapter 1

When God Speaks in the Night

From the beginning of time, God has used dreams as a divine method of communication with His people. Long before we had printed Bibles or church buildings, God was already speaking in the night. In the hands of the Creator, dreams become sacred scrolls, written by the Spirit and unsealed while we sleep.

Examples of Spiritual Dreams in Scripture

The Bible is rich with examples of God using dreams to guide, warn, reveal, and affirm. In Genesis, Joseph the dreamer was given visions that foretold his destiny and, later, the destiny of nations. His dreams caused conflict with his brothers, but they were God's way of preparing Joseph for position of influence **(Genesis 37)**.

Daniel, another gifted interpreter of dreams, relied on divine insight to decode the mysterious visions of kings. God used Daniel's dream interpretations not only to elevate him but to demonstrate His sovereignty over earthly kingdoms **(Daniel 2).**

Joseph, the earthly father of Jesus, received critical instructions in dreams.

"13 And when they were departed, behold, the angel of the Lord appeared to Joseph in a dream saying, Arise, and take the young child and his mother, and flee into Egypt, and be thou there until I bring thee word: for Herod will seek the young child to destroy him. 14 When he arose, he took the young child and his mother by night, and departed into Egypt: 15 and was there until the

death of Herod: that it might be fulfilled which was spoken of the Lord by the prophet, saying, Out of Egypt have I called my son."
Matthew 2:13-15 (KJV)

Dreams as a Tool for Intimacy and Revelation

Dreams are a language of Spirit. Unlike our waking thoughts, dreams bypass the limitation of logic and the resistance of our conscious minds. While we sleep, we are more open to receive the mysteries of God.

Spiritual dreams are like parables, symbolic, layered, and rich with meaning. Jesus often spoke in parables so that those with spiritual ears could hear. Likewise, God often hides His messages in dream imagery that invites us to seek Him for interpretation. This requires intimacy and relationship, reminding us that God doesn't just want to give us information—He wants connection. Dreams are an invitation to draw near and inquire, just as Daniel did. When we understand dreams as God's personal love letters and instructions, we stop dismissing them as random or meaningless.

The White Shirts from Heaven

As a little girl, I had a dream that visited me more than once—so vivid, so unusual, that it remained etched in my memory long after the final occurrence. In the dream, the sky above me was a brilliant blue—deep, endless, and impossibly beautiful. It wasn't like the sky I would see during the day. This sky felt alive.

And then something began to fall.

White shirts, pure and bright, descended from the heavens like soft snowflakes. They weren't tossed or thrown; they gently floated downward with quiet purpose. One by one, they began to fall on me. I didn't try to catch them. I didn't move. I simply stood there as the shirts—dozens of them— fell and covered me. Yet in this strange and serene moment, I felt something I didn't understand. **Fear.**

I always woke up immediately after, heart racing, mind spinning. Sometimes I'd just lie there, staring at the ceiling, afraid to fall back asleep.

I never told anyone.

How do you explain to someone that white shirts from the sky are haunting your dreams? That something as ordinary as clothing could feel holy, and too big for your little body to wear?

I didn't know it then, but those shirts weren't just shirts. They were something else. Something more. Now, I believe they were callings—gifts I wasn't ready to hold. Garments stitched in heaven, made for a future me.

God was trying to tell me something long before I had the language to understand it.

At that age, I had no language for dreams, no understanding of symbols, and no concept of spiritual encounters. But now, looking back with the wisdom of the Spirit and years of walking with God, I understand more clearly: that dream was not just a dream. It was a divine imprint on my destiny.

A Heavenly Dressing Room

Through Scripture, garments are powerful symbols of identity, purpose, and calling. When Joseph received his coat of many colors, it represented favor and a future. When the prodigal son returned home, the father clothed him in the best robe, a public restoration of sonship.

"I will greatly rejoice in the Lord, my soul shall be joyful in my God; for He has clothed me with the garments of salvation, He hath covered me with the robe of righteousness, as a bridegroom

decketh himself with ornaments, and as bride adorneth herself with her jewels." Isaiah 61:10 (KJV)

The white shirts in my dream were not random articles of clothing. They were **Heavenly garments,** signs of righteousness, spiritual assignments, and divine purpose. God was clothing me in what I would need to fulfill the call on my life. And He was doing it long before I could say "yes" with full understanding.

I believe the reason I felt afraid is because, even as a child, **my spirit recognized the weight** of what I was being clothed with. It's not unusual to feel unready when Heaven visits earth.

Moses turned aside in fear at the burning bush.

"2. And the angel of the Lord appeared unto him in a flame of fire out of the midst of a bush: and he looked, and, behold, the bush burned with fire, and the bush was not consumed 3. And Moses said, I will not turn aside, and see this great sight, why the bush is not burnt." Exodus 3:2-3 (KJV)

Isaiah cried out, "Woe is me!" in the presence of God.

"Woe to me!" I cried. "I am ruined" For I am a man of unclean lips, and I live among a people of unclean lips and my eyes have seen the King, the Lord Almighty." Isaiah 6:5 (NIV)

Divine encounters often come wrapped in mystery, but they leave behind undeniable marks of identity.

When Dreams Carry Identity

That dream was a glimpse into my spiritual wardrobe—a preview of what Heaven had prepared for me. I didn't realize it then, but God was already shaping me into a vessel for ministry, counseling, and healing. He was layering me in garments of purpose that I would grow into over time.

And maybe you, too, have had dreams you didn't

understand.   Recurring   images.   Mysterious moments. Feelings that lingered long after waking. Don't dismiss them. Sometimes, our dreams are not warnings or instructions but reminders. **Reminders of who we are becoming**. Of whom we already are in Christ.

Dream Reflection:

Take a moment to reflect on your own dreams.

- Have you ever had a dream where you were being given something from Heaven?

- How did it make you feel?

- Could God be revealing your identity, calling, or assignment through symbols you haven't yet interpreted?

Journal your thoughts and ask the Holy Spirit to give you understanding.

Pray the Prayer:

Father, in the Name of Jesus, thank You for clothing me in righteousness and calling me by name even before I understood who I was. I receive the garments You've prepared for me—the mantle of purpose, the robe of identity and the covering of grace. Help me to walk in what You've placed upon me and to recognize Your hand in my dreams. Teach me to discern the divine patterns in the night and to never be afraid of what comes from You. In Jesus' Name. Amen

Chapter 2

Fear of Speaking Publicly

To fulfill the call of God in my life, I had to conquer the demons in my mind. One of the biggest was the fear of public speaking.

Fear of speaking in front of others is often tied to fear of rejection, insecurity, or feeling inadequate. Scripture speaks directly to those areas. Listed are some key verses and affirmations that apply.

- *God has not given you a spirit of fear*

"For God hath not given us the spirit of fear; but of power, and of love, and of a sound mind."
2 Timothy 1:7 (KJV)

Declaration

God has not given me a spirit of fear, but of power, love, and a sound mind. I speak with clarity and confidence.

For as long as I can remember, the very thought of standing in front of people would send waves of anxiety through my body. I remember sitting in a classroom like a young girl, knowing my name would be called to present. My heart would pound in my ears, my hands would sweat, and my throat would go dry. Time and time again, I chose to take the failing grade rather than face the embarrassment of speaking in front of my peers.

- *Speak to please God, not people*

"For do I now persuade men, or God? or do I seek to please men? for if I yet please men, I should not be the servant of Christ."
Galatians 1:10 (KJV)

Declaration

I do not fear people's opinions. I speak to please God, not man.

I told myself it wasn't a big deal, that I could get by without it. But deep down, I knew fear had its grip on me.

That same fear followed me into adulthood. Even as I advanced in my career, I couldn't escape it. In 2007, I managed the Family Medical Leave Act for my job, which often required me to lead presentations and explain complex procedures. On the outside, I may have looked put together, but inside, I was silently panicking—my chest tightening, my breaths shallow, as if I was about to hyperventilate. On one occasion, my supervisor quietly took a seat at the rear of the room, drawing the employees' attention just long enough for me to catch my breath.

Side Note: "A Ram in the Bush"

Yes, the phrase "a ram in the bush" is a well-known metaphor drawn from **Genesis 22:13**, where God provided a ram as a substitute sacrifice for Isaac, but in my case (my supervisor) as a temporary substitute for me. Just as Abraham looked up and saw the ram caught in the thicket, we, too, can trust that God already has a solution prepared.

Fear is a thief. It robbed me of confidence, opportunities, and peace of mind. It made me question whether God could really use someone like me.

But God doesn't call the qualified; He qualifies the called.

- *God equips those He calls.*

"10. And Moses said unto the Lord, O my Lord, I am not eloquent, neither heretofore, nor since thou hast spoken unto thy servant: but I am slow of speech and of a slow tongue. 11. And the Lord said unto him, who hath made man's mouth? Or who maketh the dumb, or deaf, or the seeing, or the blind? have not I the Lord?

12. Now therefore go, and I will be with thy mouth, and teach tee what thou shalt say" Exodus 4:10-12 (KJV)

Moses struggled with fear and felt unqualified, but God reminded him that He would speak through him. This is a reminder that our confidence comes from God, not our own ability.

Declaration

I am chosen and called by God. He equips me and speaks through me.

Chapter 3

Overcoming Fear through Faith

In 2017, something changed. That year, I enrolled in Hope Bible Institute under the powerful teaching of Dr. Johnny B. Young Jr. It was there that I began to truly recognize my identity in Christ Jesus. The Word came alive in a new way. I started to see not just who I was but whose I was. I gained clarity on the tricks of the enemy and how he had been using fear to keep me bound. Through the power and the leading of the Holy Spirit,

Dr. Young's teaching began to unveil a profound revelation. As he spoke, it felt as though the Holy Spirit was speaking directly to me. **"And God said, let us make man in our image, after our likeness: and let them have dominion over the fish of the sea, and over the fowl of the air, and over the cattle, and over all, the earth, and over every creeping thing that creepeth upon the earth."** **Genesis 1:26 (KJV)**

Pause! and really listen to that. God said it. **"Let us make man in our image, after our likeness."** **God is Spirit, right?** So, to be made in His image means He gave us a part of Himself. He put His

Spirit—our spirit—inside of us and placed that spirit in a body made from dust, giving us a soul to possess.

At that moment, I didn't just begin to understand who I was, I began to understand whose I was. A fresh clarity came over me, and I started to recognize the subtle strategies the enemy had been using. I saw how fear had been working against me, keeping me bound to keep me silent. But once I saw the truth, fear started losing its grip.

Two scriptures that became a weapon in my arsenal were:

"For God has not given us a spirit of fear, but of power and of love and of a sound mind." 2 Timothy 1:7 (NKJV)

"I can do all things through Christ who strengthens me." Philippians 4:13 (NKJV)

I would meditate on those verses, speak them over myself, and refuse to let fear have the final word.

The transformation didn't happen overnight, but step by step, truth replaced terror. The more I stood in the confidence of who Christ said I was, the more that fear began to lose its grip. God began to give me boldness, not because I was suddenly fearless, but because I was full of faith. Looking back now, I realize the enemy tried to silence the very gift God intended to use. But the lie that I wasn't good enough, bold enough, or skilled enough could not stand against the truth of God's Word.

So, I say to you, if you're battling fear, especially the fear of stepping into your calling, know this:

"I CAN DO ALL THINGS THROUGH CHRIST WHO STRENGTHENS ME" (PHILIPPIANS 4:13, NKJV).

That includes standing, speaking, and becoming everything, He has called you to be.

The struggle was real. But so was the breakthrough.

Chapter 4

Testimonies Come After the Test

The very next year, in 2018, fresh from receiving my B.S. degree in theology, my journey took another decisive turn. Just a month after graduating, I was invited by Sister Rita Sanford to deliver a message to the ladies at North Macedonia Baptist Church in Baton Rouge, Louisiana, under the leadership of Pastor Clifton Sanford. The assignment was scheduled in only two weeks. In those brief moments before I accepted the assignment, the Holy Spirit spoke clearly to my heart: **"Obedience is better than sacrifice".**

Moving by that divine prompt, I named the message accordingly and made it the centerpiece of our teaching on the identity in Christ, beginning by praying in the spirit and inviting God's presence to fill the room and my heart completely. Every word was permeated with the boldness that comes from walking in alignment with who God said I was.

That day we didn't just deliver a message: It was a testimony to the transformative power of obedience, the reality of our identity in Christ, and the strength that flows when God calls. He equips, and when we obey, we step into the fullness of His purpose.

Standing on that podium, with the Holy Spirit echoing within me and the truth of God's Word lighting my path, I understood that every step of my struggle was a stepping stone toward purpose. My past fears were not signs of weakness but the very battles that had sharpened my faith and prepared me for the divine assignments ahead. Every moment of doubt, every jitter of anxiety, becomes a testimony of God's enduring grace—a reminder that He transforms our weakness into strength.

Today, as I reflect on my journey, I am filled with gratitude. I am grateful for every trial that taught me to lean on God, every whispered word of encouragement that spurred me on, every moment of surrender that redefined my identity. My story is a testament to the truth that when we step out in obedience, God meets us with the power, love, and clarity that drives out fear. And in that sacred act of obedience, we find that our true worth, our identity in Christ, is never defined by the things that once held us back but by the amazing grace that pushes us forward.

This is not merely my story, it is a living testimony that no matter how daunting the struggle, God's call transforms our weakness into our greatest strength, urging us to step boldly into our destiny.

"And He said to me, "My grace is sufficient for you, for My strength is made perfect in weakness." **Therefore, most gladly I will rather boast in my infirmities, that the power of Christ may rest upon me." 2 Corinthians 12:9 (NKJV)**

Weaknesses become opportunities for God's power to manifest, urging us to step boldly in the destiny He has prepared for us.

Chapter 5

A Different Kind of Encounter

Not every encounter with God comes in the form of a dream. Sometimes, He speaks through groanings, burdens, or even physical sensations that words can't explain. In 2012, something occurred in my life. I attended a revival service at Cathedral of Prayer and Deliverance, Hammond, Louisiana, under the leadership of Bishop William Cage.

Bishop called me to the altar and imparted words of wisdom over me. That moment was spiritual marking, though I didn't understand the full weight

RECOGNIZING WHEN GOD SPEAKS

of it at the time. Soon after that year, I was awakened in the night. I began to feel deep groanings in my belly. It wasn't emotional. It was spiritual and physical. Uncertain of what I was experiencing, I discerned it to be the manifested presence of the Holy Spirit and responded by praying in the Spirit. At times, the weight of His presence was so overwhelming that it felt difficult to breathe—until the Spirit lifted, signifying that the divine assignment had been fulfilled.

These moments would often happen in the night while I was asleep, and they would awaken me with a sense of urgency. I didn't always know who I was praying for, but I knew someone needed an intercessor at that moment.

Testimony: When Love Overrides

Offense

"But I say to you, love your enemies, bless those who curse you, do good to those who hate you, and pray for those who spitefully use you and persecute you..." Matthew 5:44 (NKJV)

One of the most stretching moments I've ever experienced in prayer came during the early morning hours, those "wee hours" when Holy Spirit often whispers.

I was awakened with that familiar pull in my spirit, that weight of God's presence resting heavily on me. But this time, when I asked, "Lord, who is it?" I saw the face of someone I knew…someone who didn't care for me. In fact, she had made it clear. And I had the audacity to think, "Lord, she doesn't even like me." But the Holy Spirit responded, not in words, but in weight. The burden remained.

At that moment, I understood it didn't matter who. It didn't matter what had happened or how I felt. The Lord was looking for an intercessor, not someone who needed all the details. And so, I obeyed. I began to pray in the Spirit for her. As I prayed, something in me shifted. My heart softened. The offense fell off. The burden became love.

That's when I realized: this is what it means to pray with God's heart, not mine.

"And I will give you a new heart, and I will put a new spirit in you. I will take out your stony, stubborn heart and give you a tender responsive heart." Ezekiel 36:26 (NLT)

Reflection Prompt: Praying Past the Pain

Take a moment to pause and ask:

- Has God ever brought someone to mind who hurt, rejected, or misunderstood you?

- How did you respond?

- If that happened today, would you be willing to lay aside the offense to stand in the gap for them?

Jesus didn't just pray for His friends; He prayed for those who crucified Him. Real intercession flows from His heart, not our comfort.

"Then said Jesus, Father, forgive them; for they know not what they do.**" Luke 23:34 (KJV)**

Ask the Lord to show you if there's anyone He's calling you to pray for, regardless of past pain.

It may be the very thing that sets you free, too.

Journal Your Heart-Shift Moments

Use this space to explore the times you were prompted to pray for someone you didn't expect:

Date & Time:

Who Was on Your Heart:

What Was Your Initial Reaction:

Confirmation and Obedience

One time, while watching television with my mind on Jesus, I felt His presence so strongly that I asked in my spirit, "Who is it?" And instantly, a name came to me. Days later, a prophetess, who had no idea what I had experienced, confirmed it. That was when I truly realized: God was using me as a vessel of intercession.

I started journaling each encounter, I wrote down the date, time, and the part of my body where I felt His presence. Over time, I noticed patterns and recognized Holy Spirit movement more clearly. This wasn't just for me—it was for others, and it was for God's Glory.

If you've ever felt a sudden burden, sensed a presence, or awakened with a need to pray, you're not alone. The Holy Spirit still groans through us.

Pay attention. Write it down. Ask God for clarity.

He may be using you in ways you never imagined.

Chapter 6

Testimony:

A Waking Alert:

When God Uses the Whole Body

One morning, after my usual alarm went off to prepare for work, I experienced something I'll never forget. From the moment I awoke, my entire body was gripped by an intense and unfamiliar sensation—what I could only describe as an amber alert in the spirit. It wasn't fear, but urgency. It felt as though my whole being had been placed on high alert for something critical.

As I reached for my phone, a picture appeared, an image of a little boy who needed me. At that moment, I knew exactly who the alert was for. God had used my body to carry a burden of intercession before He even revealed the face. It was a divine pairing: the sensation and the vision. Heaven had synchronized both to get my full attention.

I prayed fervently throughout the day, covering the child in protection, peace, and divine purpose. The sensation didn't lift until around 9 p.m. that night, which confirmed that this was not a passing emotion—it was an assignment. A spiritual emergency has been intercepted because God could trust me to feel it and respond.

That day taught me something I'll never forget: God doesn't just speak through dreams or visions. Sometimes, He speaks through our bodies. He bypasses the mind and alerts the spirit directly. I realized He was teaching me how to trust the unspoken language of the Spirit, to respond even when I didn't yet understand.

I've come to embrace these physical impressions

as a part of my intercessory calling. I don't always know the details in the moment, but I do know this: when God awakens your body with urgency, He is trusting you with heaven's business. That kind of trust is sacred.

"The spirit of man *is* the candle of the Lord, Searching all the inward parts of the belly." Proverbs 20:27 (KJV)

"But the Comforter, *which is* the Holy Ghost, whom the Father will send in my name, he shall teach you all things, and bring all things to your remembrance, whatsoever I have said unto you." John 14:26 (KJV)

Let's Pray

Father, In the Name of Jesus, thank You for divine sensitivity You've placed within me. I honor the times You alert me through my body, trusting me with Your intercessory calling. Help me to respond in obedience, even when I don't fully understand. Teach me to discern the times, the needs, and the people You are calling me to intercede for. May my spirit remain aligned with Yours, and may Your will be accomplished through my prayers. In Jesus' Name, Amen.

Reflection Prompt

Take a moment to reflect:

- Have you ever felt an unexplainable burden or stirring in your spirit, especially during the night or early morning?

- Was there a moment when you felt God's presence strongly in your body without knowing why at first?

- Did you later find out the reason or are you still waiting for understanding?

Ask the Holy Spirit to bring clarity and confirmation. He may be showing you that He's calling you into a deeper level of intercession.

Journal Your Burden Moments

Use this space to begin documenting your own experiences. Ask the Holy Spirit to remind you of times when He moves through you in groaning, urgency, or even discomfort.

Date:

Time of day:

Where You Felt in Your Body:

What You Were Doing at the Time:

Who or What Came to Mind (if anyone):

As you journal, remember: These entries are not just memories, they are spiritual records. God honors what you write, and over time, you'll begin to recognize patterns in how He speaks to you.

Chapter 7

When the Air Speaks

Discerning the Smoke

There are moments when God speaks not through words but through the atmosphere. What lingers in the air becomes a divine alert and invisible message demanding spiritual attention.

I've encountered this experience twice, and both times it touched me in a way I'll never forget.

The First Encounter:

A Sweet Yet Burning Reminder

It began on September 6, 2021, Labor Day. I was at my sister's house in Georgia for a family gathering. People stepped outside to smoke, so when I first caught a whiff of cigarette smoke, I thought nothing of it. But the scent didn't leave. In fact, it followed me. It showed up in places where no smoke should've been, in my car, in my bed, at work. Sometimes it was a sweet, almost pleasant cigar aroma, and other times it stung and burned my nostrils like fire.

I was puzzled. I checked everything; was something physically wrong? Was there a spiritual root? I prayed constantly, seeking understanding. Was this another level of spiritual sensitivity? A new dimension of discernment? I cried out to God: "What are You showing me?"

Then I felt prompted to release a message on social media. It was simple: a call for anyone battling with the spirit of nicotine to join in a prayer for deliverance. To my surprise, the very next day, the smell began to lift. Gradually, it disappeared completely. By December 18, 2021, it was gone.

The Second Encounter:

A Triple Warning

Years passed, and on March 15, 2025, the smell returned, but this time, it intensified and diversified. I began smelling not one, but three distinct types of smoke:

- **Nicotine smoke**, just like before

- **Incense,** which brought a false sense of peace but was spiritually troubling

- **Burning Trash,** a harsh, nauseating scent that lingered like judgment

As I meditated and sought the Lord, I was reminded of a vision I'd once seen of trash pails lined up in front of homes, uncollected, symbolic of things not yet dealt with.

The Lord impressed upon me the importance of releasing this message to the Body of Christ. Each of these types of smoke carried meaning and toxicity:

- **Nicotine Smoke** represents addiction and physical destruction. It damages the lungs, heart, and blood vessels.

- **Incense Smoke,** while often used in spiritual practices, has been linked to health risks and can represent strange fire, worship or practices that are not of God.

- **Burning Trash** is symbolic of toxic waste, things that should've been thrown out but are now causing harm. It represents unaddressed issues, hidden sins, and environmental and spiritual pollution.

These smells were spiritual signals. They weren't just about the physical act of smoking or burning; they were about spiritual toxicity, what we allow into our lives, what we tolerate, and what needs to be dealt with.

We are not called to condemn anyone. But we are called to intercede.

Let Us Pray

Father God, in the Name of Jesus, lift every person battling addiction, bound by the spirit of smoke exposure, whether nicotine, incense, or environmental toxins. Lord, You are our Deliverer. I declare in the Name of Jesus to

destroy every stronghold, every generational curse, and every demonic influence associated with smoke. In the mighty name of Jesus, we declare freedom. We command the grip of addiction and deception to break now and return to the pit of hell. Lord, release Your ministering angels to bring healing, clarity, and restoration. Renew minds and hearts. Let Your fresh wind blows and purify every soul affected. We decree deliverance, healing, and wholeness in Jesus' Name.

Amen

Reflection:

The Fragrance of Discernment

- Have you ever sensed something in your environment that had no natural explanation?

- Could God be trying to get your attention through your senses?

- What "uncollected trash" might be lingering in your spiritual life or community?

- How can you intercede for those struggling with hidden battles?

As you meditate, ask the Holy Spirit to increase your discernment, not just to see and hear but to sense the atmosphere. Just as smoke carries a scent, so do spirits carry a presence. Not everything that smells good is from God, and not everything unpleasant is meant to harm Sometimes, it's meant to awaken.

"Now thanks be to God, who always leads us in triumph in Christ, and through us diffuses the fragrance of His knowledge in every place. For we are to God the fragrance of Christ among those who are being saved and among those who are perishing." 2 Corinthians 2:14-15 (NJKV)

Chapter 8

Power of Meditation in God's Presence

Early one morning during meditation, I sensed these words in my spirit: **"Set aside one hour for meditation from 6 a.m. to 7 a.m."** This hour is to be a time of sacrificial posture before the Lord, quiet, surrendered, and focused on Him. The atmosphere should be set with instrumental music only.

There will be no preaching and no audible prayers, just stillness in His presence. Though we will gather corporately, this will be a deeply personal, individual encounter with God.

Another Way God Speaks:

Through Meditation

One of the most overlooked but deeply powerful ways God speaks is through meditation. We often expect God to speak through dreams, prophecy, or a sermon — and He does. But there are times when His voice comes not through noise, but through stillness.

Meditation is not simply quiet time — it is God-focused stillness. It is where our spirit tunes in to hear His whisper, our hearts slow down to receive His direction, and our minds reflect on His Word until it becomes alive within us. Through meditation, revelation often rises.

"Be still, and know that I am God; I will be exalted among the nations, I will be exalted in the earth!." Psalm 46:10 (KJV)

What is Meditation?

Meditation, in the biblical context, is the act of intentionally focusing the heart and mind on God —

His Word, His presence, His character, and His voice. Unlike the world's version that often involves emptying the mind, godly meditation is about filling the mind with truth, aligning our spirit with the Holy Spirit, and quieting distractions so we can commune with the Father.

Joshua 1:8 (NKJV) gives us a foundation:

"This Book of the Law shall not depart from your mouth, but you shall meditate on it day and night, that you may observe to do according to all that is written in it. For then you will make your way prosperous, and then you will have good success."

Biblical Meditation Involves:

- Focused attention on God's Word

- Deep reflection on His ways

- Intentional stillness to hear His voice.

Did Jesus Meditate or Pray?

When we read the Gospels, the word most often used for Jesus' time with the Father is prayer. But if we look closer at how He prayed, we see practices that align with what we call meditation today.

Jesus' Pattern of Stillness:

"But Jesus often withdrew to lonely places and prayed." (Luke 5:16 NIV)

"Very early in the morning, while it was still dark, Jesus got up, left the house and went off to a solitary place, where he prayed." (Mark 1:36 NIV)

"One of those days Jesus went out to a mountainside to pray, and spent the night praying to God." (Luke 6:12 NIV)

These moments were not rushed. They were intentional times of solitude, quietness, and communion with the Father. He wasn't simply reciting words; He was engaging deeply—listening, aligning, and receiving strength.

Prayer vs Meditation:

- **Prayer** is often expressive — talking to God, presenting requests, giving thanks.

- **Meditation** is receptive — reflecting on God's Word, listening for His voice, and being still before Him.

Jesus demonstrated both. He prayed with words, but His extended times of silence and withdrawal reveal a posture of meditative communion.

Why This Matters:

If Jesus, the Son of God, needed moments of silence to reconnect with the Father, how much more do we? His life teaches us that stillness is not optional for those who want clarity and power. Meditation is simply the practice of doing what Jesus modeled: slowing down, listening, and aligning with God's heart.

Personal Reflection: Meditation as a Lefestyle

Before the Lord spoke to me, I was reminded of Jesus at the wedding in Cana — His first recorded miracle. **"He turned water into wine" John 2:1–11 (NIV).**

I smiled at the thought: "Lord, You turned water into wine, if only I could turn wine back into water!"

As I began driving, I leaned into meditation — quietly communing with the Lord, listening. Suddenly, I heard Him speak clearly to my spirit:

"There will be free alcohol for about 100 people. Your assignment is to pray over it — that no one becomes intoxicated or disrupts the celebration."

When I arrived, at the venue, very few people showed up. Suddenly, the bartender approached me — assuming I was in charge — and asked, "Where's the alcohol?"

I knew this was my moment.

Before handing her the bottles, I paused. I turned to her and said, "Wait." Then, one by one, I placed my hands on each bottle and prayed in the name of Jesus: "They will not get drunk." I declared peace over the reception, protection over every guest, and order in the atmosphere. The Spirit of God was all over that moment. And guess what? Not one person became intoxicated. The reception flowed with joy, celebration, and peace. The Spirit of God had gone before — because of meditation.

Meditation Prepares Us for

Divine Assignments

Just like Jesus withdrew to solitary places to pray and receive instruction from the Father, we too must develop a rhythm of intentional meditation. His time alone wasn't just for rest — it was strategic preparation. **"1 Jesus, full of the Holy Spirit, left the Jordan and was led by the Spirit into the wilderness, 2 where for forty days he was tempted by the devil. 14 Jesus returned to Galilee in the power of the Spirit. And news about him spread through the whole countryside." Luke 4:1–2, 14 (NIV)**

"So Jesus said to them, Truly, truly, I say to you, the Son can do nothing of his own accord, but only what he sees the Father doing. For whatever the Father does, that the Son does likewise**." John 5:19 (ESV)**

"Let me hear of your unfailing love each morning, for I am trusting you. Show me where to walk, for I give myself to you." Psalm 143:8 (NLT)

"In all your ways acknowledge Him, and He shall direct your paths." Proverbs 3:6 (NKJV)

RECOGNIZING WHEN GOD SPEAKS

Those who Meditated Before Us

- Isaac –

"And Isaac went out to meditate in the field at the eventide: and he lifted his eyes, and saw, and behold, the camels were coming." Genesis 24:63 (KJV)

Hebrew word for "meditate" here is "suach" implying musing, meditating, or even conversing.

Isaac meditated to seek God's presence, reflect on his life's direction, and prepare his heart for the new relationship he was about to enter.

2. David –

"But his delight is in the law of the Lord. and on his law, he meditates day and night." Psalms 1:2 (ESV)

Hebrew word for "meditate" here is "hagah." It implies meditate, study, utter.

David meditated on God's Word because he delighted in it. Meditation was a response to love; it wasn't a duty but a joy. He longed to stay spiritually rooted and fruitful, and meditating on the Word kept him connected to God's will.

"When I remember You on my bed, I meditate on You in the night watches." Psalms 63:6" (ESV)

The Hebrew word for "meditate" here is "hagah." It implies to murmur, ponder, imagine, meditate, mourn.

David is in the wilderness, fleeing enemies. He meditated during lonely, vulnerable moments—at night, when fear and uncertainty might creep in. His meditation was an act of worship and trust. Instead of rehearsing anxiety, he rehearsed God's faithfulness.

"Oh, how I love Your law! It is my meditation all the day" Psalms 119:97 (ESV)

The Hebrew word for "meditation" here is "siychah." It implies extension, devotion, meditation, prayer.

David expresses love for God's Word. Meditation was his way of keeping God at the center of everything. It helped him align his thoughts, actions, and emotions with truth. This wasn't a casual reflection; it was continual, intentional focus throughout his day.

3. Joshua –

"This book of the law shall not depart out of thy mouth, but thou shalt meditate therein day and night, that thou mayest observe to do according to all that is written therein: for then thou shalt make thy way prosperous and then thou shalt have good success." Joshua 1:8 (KJV)

Joshua meditated so he could lead with wisdom, walk in obedience, experience God's success, and remain strong and courageous. Meditation was not optional; it was essential for victory.

4. **Mary Mother of Jesus -**

"But Mary treasured up all these things, pondering them in her heart." Luke 2:19 (ESV)

Mary meditated on the words and events surrounding Jesus' birth. She didn't rush to speak; she reflected deeply, storing up spiritual truths.

Reflection Questions

☐ 1. Have you recognized God's voice more clearly during moments of stillness or meditation? Describe one of those times.

☐ 2. What does your current rhythm of meditation look like — or is God calling you to begin one?

☐ 3. What environments (like driving, sitting outside, journaling) help you meditate best on God's presence or Word?

☐ 4. Has the Holy Spirit ever given you an assignment while meditating? What was your response?

☐ 5. Is there a Scripture God keeps bringing to your heart? What is He saying through it?

☐ 6. What steps can you take this week to make more space for divine stillness?

Let's Pray

Father, thank You for inviting me into the stillness where Your voice becomes clear. Teach me to slow down and rest in Your presence. Help me make space for You — not just in quiet rooms, but in everyday moments. Train my spirit to recognize Your whispers. Let Your Word be my meditation day and night. Give me ears to hear, a heart to obey, and the courage to act. In Jesus' name.

Amen.

Declaration

I declare that I am one who meditates in the presence of God.

His Word is alive in me.

His voice is clear to me.

His assignments are revealed to me in the stillness.

I do not rush — I rest.

I do not fear — I focus.

And I do not miss my moment — I move when He speaks.

Meditation is not just what I do — it is who I am.

I live, move, and have my being in Him.

Prompts for Meditation: Expanded and Reflective

1. "What does it mean for God's Word not to depart from my mouth?"

Reflect on:

• Am I regularly speaking the Word of God, or is my speech filled with fear, doubt, or worldly language?

• Do I declare God's promises over my life, family, ministry, and purpose?

• What confessions of faith do I need to keep on my lips daily?

Meditative Action:

• Start your day by speaking aloud a scripture that agrees with what you're trusting God to do in your life.

• Speak God's Word as a sword against fear, lack, or uncertainty.

"Death and life are in the power of the tongue: And they that love it shall eat the fruit thereof." (Proverbs. 18:21 KJV)

2. "How can I meditate day and night as a lifestyle?"

Reflect on:

• What thoughts fill my mind during quiet moments—worry, stress, or the Word?

• Do I schedule time to meditate, or do I only read the Bible when it's convenient?

• Are there scriptural truths I can carry into my morning and nighttime routines?

Meditative Action:

• Establish a rhythm: Morning meditation for direction, evening meditation for reflection and release.

• Choose one verse a day to ruminate on. Keep it on a note card, phone screen, or journal.

Like chewing cud, biblical meditation involves mentally returning to God's truth over and over until it nourishes your spirit.

3. "What areas in my life need the success promised through obedience?"

Reflect on:

• Are there any areas in my life—relationships, ministry, business, health—where I feel stuck or lacking direction?

• Have I obeyed what God last told me to do?

• Is my definition of "success" aligned with God's?

Meditative Action:

• Ask the Holy Spirit: "What area of my life needs to come into alignment with Your Word?"

• Journal what He reveals.

• Search for scriptures that speak into those areas and begin confessing and obeying them.

RECOGNIZING WHEN GOD SPEAKS

Success in God's Kingdom is the fruit of obedience, not ambition. Meditation aligns your steps with His will.

Bonus Prompt: "Am I meditating on truth or trauma?"

Reflect on:

• What thoughts dominate my mind daily?

• Do I replay past pain, offense, and failure—or do I replay God's truth, healing, and promises?

• Have I allowed old wounds to shape my inner narrative more than God's Word?

Meditative Action:

• Identify a painful narrative you've rehearsed.

• Replace it with a healing scripture.

• Speak it out loud until it replaces your inner monologue.

Romans 12:2 reminds that transformation begins by renewing the mind—meditation is the process that renews.

"And be not conformed to this world: but be ye transformed by the renewing of your mind, that ye may prove what *is* that good, and acceptable, and perfect, will of God." Romans 12:2(KJV)

Chapter 9

When Heaven Sings – Hearing God Through Lyrics

Foundation

"Speaking to yourselves in psalms and hymns and spiritual songs, singing and making melody in your heart to the Lord." Ephesians 5:19 (KJV)

"Let the word of Christ dwell in you richly in all wisdom; teaching and admonishing one another in psalms and hymns and spiritual songs, singing with grace in your hearts to the Lord." Col 3:16 (KJV)

"Yet the Lord will command his lovingkindness in the daytime, and in the night his song shall be with me, and my prayer unto the God of my life." Psalm 42:8 (KJV)

The Lord thy God in the midst of thee is mighty; he will save, he will rejoice over thee with joy; he will rest in his love, he will joy over thee with singing. Zephaniah 3:17 (KJV)

Reflection

Have you ever awakened with a song playing in your spirit, as if the melody came from somewhere beyond sleep? Or maybe throughout your day, a lyric suddenly rises within you, words that seem to speak directly to your situation. That's not random. It could be the Holy Spirit echoing God's voice through spiritual lyrics.

God's Word affirms that He speaks through psalms, hymns, and spiritual songs. These are not just forms of worship, they are vehicles of divine communication.

Sometimes, a lyric carries more than encouragement—it carries instruction, conviction, warning, or healing.

The same Spirit who inspired Scripture also inspires the songs that align with it. If a lyric sticks with you, don't ignore it. Pause and ask:

"Lord, what are You trying to say to me through this?"

Journal Prompts

1. What lyrics or songs have recently been repeated in your mind or heart?

2. Does the message of that lyric line up with Scripture?

3. What might God be encouraging, convicting, or reminding you of?

4. How can you respond in prayer or action to that message?

Let's Pray

Father, thank You for singing over me and speaking to me in ways that are tender, personal, and unexpected. Help me to recognize Your voice, even in the songs that rise in my spirit. Teach me to pause, listen, and obey what You're saying—whether through the written Word or through spiritual songs. I open my ears and heart to Your melody. In Jesus' name.

Amen.

Divine Echoes: Biblical Examples of Lyrics from Heaven

While the Bible may not describe someone waking up with a modern worship song in their head, it is rich with examples of God speaking through music, lyrics, and prophetic songs. From David's psalms to the heavenly choir at Christ's birth, God has long used melody to convey His message.

David – The Psalmist and Lyricist of Heaven

David is perhaps the most well-known biblical example of someone who received spiritual songs.

His psalms were not merely poetic expressions, but prophetic lyrics inspired by encounters with God. David testifies: **"And he hath put a new song in my mouth, even praise unto our God: Many shall see it, and fear, and shall trust in the Lord." Psalm 40:3 (KJV)**

These songs often emerged from worship, warfare, or divine revelation.

These leaders received lyrics that carried revelation, correction, and comfort.

Paul Encouraging Spiritual Songs

In the New Testament, Paul encourages believers to speak in psalms and hymns. He confirms that

Spirit-led lyrics are part of Christian life and communication—another avenue through which God speaks today.

"Speaking to ourselves in psalms and hymns and spiritual songs, singing and making melody in your heart to the Lord." Ephesians 5:19 (KJV)

Chapter 10

When God Speaks Through Prayer and Intercession

One of the most intimate and powerful ways I've recognized the voice of God is during prayer and intercession. His whisper has come unexpectedly, yet precisely, while simply seeking Him on behalf of others.

I remember one particular moment during a prophetic class. The Apostle leading the session gave us an assignment: before the course concluded, each participant would prophecy to someone in the room.

After the first meeting, I began to ask the Holy Spirit to reveal something about a fellow classmate. But to my surprise, the Lord revealed something deeply personal about the Apostle herself. I hesitated, unsure whether to speak, so I shared what I sensed through a private text message. Her response left me in awe—she confirmed that I had no natural way of knowing what I shared. It was a divine revelation that spoke directly to her life and brought great encouragement. I give all glory to God.

"Call to me and I will answer you and will tell you great and hidden things that you have not known." Jeremiah 33:3 (ESV)

Another time, while preparing to counsel someone in a scheduled meeting, I began to intercede on their behalf. Twice, the Lord interrupted my prayers and redirected me toward another couple. I didn't understand the shift, but I obeyed. That evening, the original meeting was unexpectedly cancelled but I later discovered that the couple I had interceded for needed urgent spiritual covering. I didn't know the details, but God did.

"In the same way, the Spirit helps us in our weakness. We do not know what we ought to pray for, but the Spirit himself intercedes for us through wordless groans." Romans 8:26 (NIV)

These experiences continue to remind me that prayer is more than conversation, it's divine communication. Intercession is not just about speaking to God; it's about listening to Him. When we surrender our agendas in prayer, He reveals His.

"My sheep hear My voice, and I know them, and they follow Me." John 10:27 (NKJV)

Reflection & Journal Prompts with Scripture

Use the following prompts to reflect on how God may be speaking to you during your own times of prayer and intercession.

1. When was the last time you sensed God speaking to you while praying?

☐ Write about what you sensed and how you responded.

"The Lord is near to all who call on him, to all who call on him in truth." —Psalm 145:18 (NIV)

2. Have you ever prayed for someone and later learned they needed it at that exact moment?

☐ What confirmation did you receive that it was a God moment?

"Before they call, I will answer; while they are still speaking, I will hear." —Isaiah 65:24 (NIV)

3. Has God ever redirected your focus in prayer like He did with me?

☐ Reflect on the shift. What did you learn from the redirection?

"Trust in the Lord with all your heart and lean not on your own understanding..." — Proverbs 3:5 (NIV)

4. Is there someone the Lord is bringing to your heart to pray for today?

☐ Pause now. Write their name, pray, and journal what comes to your spirit.

"Devote yourselves to prayer, being watchfu and thankful." —Colossians 4:2 (NIV)

5. What holds you back from sharing when God speaks to you about someone else?

☐ Journal about any fears or concerns and surrender them in prayer.

"For God has not given us a spirit of fear, but of power and of love and of a sound mind." — **2 Timothy 1:7 (NKJV)**

6. Write a prayer of surrender:

☐ "Lord, I yield my heart and ears to hear You more clearly in prayer. Speak, and I will listen."

"The Lord came and stood there, calling as at the other times, "Samuel! Samuel!" Then Samuel said, "Speak, for your servant is listening." 1 Samuel 3:10 (NIV)

Chapter 11

Ashes to Glory

A Father's Prophetic Word

Confirmed

Jeremiah 1:5 (NLT)

"I knew you before I formed you in your mother's womb. Before you were born, I set you apart and appointed you as my prophet to the nations."

Several months before my father, J.C. Jackson, transitioned to be with the Lord, he looked at me and spoke words I wasn't ready to receive: "You're going to be a preacher." I brushed it off and quietly mumbled, "Not me," with no intention of embracing the weight of what he spoke.

After his farewell celebration and my return home, I was still carrying the weight of grief and reflection. I laid down to rest—and it was in that moment of stillness that God met me. As I awakened, I saw something truly unexpected: radiant, colorful sparkles falling gently from the ceiling onto my body. They were vibrant, glowing, and so tangible that I screamed from fear and confusion.

But as I caught my breath and gathered my thoughts, something powerful settled in my spirit.

The sparkles reminded me of my father. He had requested to be cremated, and as I looked at those glittering lights, it felt as though God was turning ashes into glory. That moment became sacred—an unspoken confirmation that my father's prophetic word wasn't just a suggestion. It was a divine call. More than sparkles, it was a mantle. A spiritual transfer.

What once rested on my father was now falling on me, not in the form of fabric, but in the form of lights. It was the confirmation of the call he had spoken over me, and at that moment, I could no longer deny it.

Holy Spirit was speaking. The call to preach had already been spoken by a father—and now, it was being confirmed by the Father.

Spiritual Reflection

God often uses those closest to us to plant seeds of destiny. Sometimes, we don't recognize the weight of their words until God Himself breathes on them again.

My father's voice carried more than love—it carried legacy. And God, in His kindness, brought a heavenly confirmation through something as gentle and surprising as sparkles from above. What once frightened me became the very moment understood: the call of God had always been on my life.

When the Spirit of God speaks, He often echoes what has already been declared through legacy, through love, and through those who saw us before we saw ourselves.

Scriptures for Meditation

"And in the last days it shall be, God declares, that I will pour out my Spirit on all flesh, and your sons and your daughters shall prophesy, and your young men shall se visions, and your old men shall dream dreams:" Acts 2:17 (ESV)

"to appoint unto them that mourn in Zion, to give unto them beauty for ashes, the oil of joy for mourning, the garment of praise for the spirit of heaviness; that they might be called tress of righteousness, the planting of the Lord, that He might be glorified." Isaiah 61:3 (KJV)

Reflection Questions

1. Has someone ever spoken over your life in a way you didn't understand at the time?

2. Can you identify a moment when God used a supernatural sign to confirm His call?

3. How might God be using your family history or legacy to affirm your purpose?

Let's Pray

Father, thank You for those who see in us what we sometimes fail to recognize. Thank You for confirming Your word in such personal, undeniable ways. I receive the calling You placed on my life—even when I once resisted it. Let my life bring You glory as I walk in obedience to the legacy You've entrusted to me. In Jesus' name.

Amen.

Declaration

I receive the call of God on my life. What once felt like ashes, God is turning into glory. I am chosen, I am called, and I will fulfill the purpose spoken over me, both on Earth as it is in heaven.

Chapter 12

"Keep Listening: A Life Led by His Voice"

"My sheep hear My voice, and I know them, and they follow Me." John 10:27 (KJV)

As we bring this journey to a close, remember—this is only the beginning of a deeper, ongoing relationship with the One who speaks. *Recognizing When God Speaks* is not a destination; it's a lifestyle. It's waking up each day with your spiritual ears tuned in and your heart open, expecting to hear from the Father, who loves you more than words can express.

You Are Being Trained to Reign

Everything you've read, prayed, and pondered in these pages has been part of God's divine training. He's been fine-tuning your ability to recognize His presence—in dreams, in prayer, in Scripture, through spiritual sensations, and even through lyrics or silence. He is teaching you to reign in life, led by revelation not just information.

You may not always get it perfect. Sometimes you'll question what you hear. That's okay. The Lord is patient. He celebrates your willingness to seek Him.

Reflections

Take a few moments to reflect on what you've learned. Consider these questions:

1. What was the clearest moment in your life when you knew God spoke?

2. What senses or signs do you now recognize as part of His communication with you?

3. How will you keep your spirit sensitive to His voice daily?

4. Who in your life needs to hear what you've now received?

Let's Prayer

Heavenly Father, Thank You for awakening my spirit and teaching me to recognize Your voice. I yield my heart, my mind, and my soul to be fully led by You. Let every whisper of Your Spirit shape my life. I declare that I walk in clarity, not confusion. I embrace divine interruptions as opportunities for alignment. And I will no longer doubt when You speak—I will listen and obey. In Jesus' name. Amen.

Your Invitation

If you've encountered God in a new way through this book, I'd love to hear from you. Share your testimony or connect with me personally at

jacquattajj@gmail.com

Join us at our next gathering for: **Power of Meditation i** **God's Presence**

Stay updated by emailing us for following upcoming event details.

Let's continue the journey—together.

ABOUT THE AUTHOR

Dr. Jacquatta J. Jones is an ordained minister of the Gospel, a licensed professional Christian therapist, and a passionate advocate for spiritual growth and inner healing. She is the devoted wife of Apostle Tony Jones, both founders of Restoration Counseling Agency, and together they serve the Kingdom through counseling, teaching, and ministry.

As the founder of Crochet Hair Creation, LLC, Dr. Jones blends creativity with purpose, encouraging others to embrace both their spiritual and natural identity. Her deep understanding of the power of meditation in God's presence was birthed during a sacred moment when the Lord spoke to her in quiet reflections.

Dr. Jones has a heart for those who are spiritually curious, questioning their purpose, and hungry for more of God. Through personal experiences and divine encounters, she helps readers recognize when God is speaking, interpret spiritual messages, and receive revelation from Scripture. Her ministry is marked by a desire to see others walk boldly in their God-given identity and purpose.

If you're interested in joining believers to meditate in the presence of God for one hour, feel free to contact her at jacquattajj@gmail.com

www.ingramcontent.com/pod-product-compliance
Lightning Source LLC
Chambersburg PA
CBHW071514120626
46550CB00006B/2221